THIS BEAUTIFUL EARTH

WILL PARFITT

D1827710

Will Parfitt has explored personal and spiritual development for more than forty years. Trained in Psychosynthesis and a Kabbalah teacher, Will lives in Glastonbury, England. He can be contacted via his website:

www.willparfitt.com

other books currently available
by the same author

FICTION
The Great Circle of Time

KABBALAH
The Complete Guide to the Kabbalah
Kabbalah: The Tree of Life
The New Kabbalah For Life

PSYCHOLOGY
Psychosynthesis: The Elements and Beyond
Walking Through Walls
The Elements of Psychosynthesis
Psychosynthesis: New Perspectives (editor)
The Something and Nothing of Death

THIS BEAUTIFUL EARTH

Gardening as a Spiritual Practice

WILL PARFITT

PS AVALON
Glastonbury, England

First published in the U.K. in 2016 by PS Avalon

PS Avalon
BM Synthesis
London, WC1N 3XX, U.K.
www.willparfitt.com

Will Parfitt asserts the moral right
to be identified as the author of this work

Design: Will Parfitt

ISBN 978-0-9572246-7-4

DEDICATION

To all the people in my life
who have demonstrated how to garden,
both literally and with a spiritual approach,
including George, Jim, Dot, Paul, Adam,
Chris, Geoff, Ark, and especially Patti

CONTENTS

INTRODUCTION

Life requires a balance between having a vision for how you want your relationship with the earth to be and a willingness to accept things as they are, not necessarily as you want them to be. Gardening is no different, so how we relate to our garden mirrors how we relate to life, and vice versa.

Work in the garden is a co-operative process in action. We are always co-operating, nature and us. This beautiful earth is a living being with its thoughts, feelings, sensations and insights … it is something that evolves with a life of its own. A gardener is part of the garden and the relationship between the garden and gardener is a shared practice of mindful living, of increasing consciousness.

This book contains many stories that have a spiritual take on gardening. You may recognize some of them as adaptations from Zen koans, Sufi stories about Mullah Nasruddin, Taoist teachings, even popular jokes from different cultures. All these stories can connect you to a deeper, older archetypal rhythm, the rhythm of nature and the earth herself, something collective that we grasp when we put our hands deep into the soil – or should that be soul?

The mindful, aware gardener approaches a garden as a pilgrim on a journey of discovery, not as a missionary who knows everything beforehand. The garden then becomes this beautiful earth in which each of us lives and grows in a continuing journey of exploration.

The gardener referred to in this book is someone who tends a garden but not necessarily someone who has an actual, physical garden. The gardener is a metaphor for the Self, that part of us that observes, witnesses without judgment and, through its connection to our deepest sense of conscience, helps us make affirmative decisions in life.

The quotes at the beginning of each chapter are from the poetry of Andrew Marvell.

IN LEAGUE WITH THE EARTH

"How could such sweet and wholesome hours
Be reckoned but with herbs and flowers!"

When the gardener returned to her house one day, she surprised a burglar in the living room. The burglar went to defend himself, as if the gardener might attack him.

"No, no," said the gardener, "do not be alarmed. Thank you for visiting my humble home."

Picking up several CDs from a nearby pile, she offered them to the dumb-struck burglar. "Here," she said, "you must not leave empty-handed."

Snatching the CDs, the burglar ran out of the house and down the street.

"Poor guy!" said the gardener, looking out of the window at her garden. "I wish I could have given him this beautiful earth."

The gardener could not give the garden to the thief because he would not have had any idea how to tend it. Any garden, however small, however large, needs tending. Even if somehow the thief could get the garden in his swag bag and carry it away, he could not steal the relationship that is at the heart of tending a garden.

In the Bible, in the Book of Job it says: 'you will be in league with the stones of the field, and the beasts of the field will be at peace with you.' To be in league with the earth means to remember that any particular plot or garden – indeed, any place where you are – is one little piece of the whole planet Earth.

Soil is composed of small particles and little stones and rotting composting stuff, and whatever the gardener has added to it. It is also home for earthworms, ants, beetles, spiders, many different creatures you might see; and microbes, soil bacteria, thrips, and many little creatures you never see. Their eco-system is your garden. To make no split between ecology and spirituality in your life and in your gardening means to value nature as you value your very soul.

When you are at war with yourself you cannot be at peace with the garden. Conversely, however – and rather wonderfully – if you make yourself at peace within the garden, a truce is called between your inner warring factions. They may go back to war later, but for now they will be receptive to what the garden tells them. And the garden always tells them the same thing: to remain in league with the earth.

FALLEN LEAVES

"Annihilating all that's made
To a green thought in a green shade."

The gardener said: "Fallen leaves do not rise up and return to the branches. To try to make them do so would be pointless."

COMMENT

Fallen leaves make leaf mould. They provide sustenance for fungi that slowly rot their structure. Layer the leaves, water them, stamp on them, and in two to three years you have leaf mould.

Leaf mould can provide nutrition for soils; it can be used as excellent mulch; it will help the soil retain moisture and keep the weeds under control.

It will also help trees to grow, trees on which leaves will develop. In their own way – with your co-operation – the fallen leaves will have risen up and returned to the branches.

THE SEASONS

"For when the sun the grass hath vexed,
The tawny mowers enter next."

One day a priest stopped to admire a beautiful garden. He spoke to the gardener. "What wonderful work you and God have done together in creating this garden!' he exclaimed.

"Yes," replied the gardener, "thank you. And you should have seen it when God was tending it on his own."

Nothing happens in isolation. The gardener is as an ally who co-operates with the evolution of both herself and the world around her. The whole process of evolution is one of co-creation as what we do affects our world and our world affects us.

When you are absent from your garden in spring, weeds grow and you risk them taking over. You risk new little plantlets being baked dry. When you are absent in the autumn, the dead leaves pile up, lettuces may run to seed and you risk a return to chaos. When you are absent from your garden, all is deserted, alone. Once more it is nature's garden. Yet when you return, you do not send nature away, or impose upon her, you find ways to co-operate again. In a garden you cannot work against the seasons.

In the film 'Being There' Peter Sellers plays a simple gardener who has always lived inside the walls of a rich man's house, tending the garden and knowing nothing of the world. One day the owner dies and 'Chancey Gardener' enters, for the first time, the 'real world' of the city. Through a series of events, he becomes the confidant of a dying billionaire who advises the president. Chancey's simple truisms are taken as meaningful metaphors that can be applied to all walks of life and by the end of the movie he is to become president.

So what is this wisdom that takes him to this elevated position? Basically, that in a garden you cannot work against the seasons. "Spring is a time for planting"; "after fall we have winter, then spring returns again". In this simplicity is the greatest wisdom. It is the key to happiness and success in a garden and on this beautiful earth.

"There birds sing consorts, garlands grow,
Cool winds do whisper, springs do flow."

The gardener smiled. "The yellow flowers are of themselves yellow flowers; the brown earth is of itself brown earth," she said.

COMMENT

The kestrel roams the sky, hovering like a giant insect before swooping down on smaller animals for food. An ant fulfils its potential through its size, its cleverness and its regimentation.

No kestrel ever wants to be an ant and ants do not want to be birds. Only the gardener can harbour fantasies, dissatisfactions, self-deceptions, try to be something she is not, and have ideals that cannot be reached.

Remain clear, feel satisfied, accept what is happening in the garden, allow yourself to be just what you are, and let the course of nature run concurrently with your intent for the garden.

The pink flowers are of themselves pink flowers. The gardener is of him or herself a gardener. How to be this gardener who lives in tune with the spirits of nature?

Just one sniff of a deep red rose and the whole world is fragrant.

THE FOUR QUALITIES

"Where men like grasshoppers appear,
But grasshoppers are giants there."

The gardener turned a rock over in the garden and remembered a saying attributed to Jesus: "Smite the rock and you will find me there; cleave the wood and there am I."

It's all in there, relatively, she mused, as she attended to the elements of her gardening, what was visible and what was waiting to become visible.

COMMENT

The four qualities involved in the art of gardening are harmony, respect, purity and peacefulness. Indeed, these are the four qualities inherent in any spiritual practice.

Harmony refers to the relationship between the gardener and the garden. Respect is what the gardener has for all the living creatures, from the carefully tended rose bush to the pesky bindweed. We are all created equal in the garden. This is not to counsel inactivity, but respect. The love of the greater whole may necessitate choice, division, uprooting. We do this with respect.

Part of the relationship between the gardener and the garden that should not be overlooked is the more difficult feelings and emotions. Gardening can bring up anger and struggle as much as it can bring up joy and peacefulness. All these feelings have to be respected and included for true harmony to be manifest. Harmony is not found in perfection, or striving for such. Harmony is found within being with what is, and making one's choices from this place. The garden is then a container or vessel for all the projections the garden experiences. They are reflected back with tranquillity and purity.

Purity is in the body of the gardener and in the body of the garden and engages the mind and feelings of all who enter the garden. This attitude is without competition, enmity with nature, desire to use things instead of having them be. Purity is lost when anything is wanted. It is present when things are allowed to be. Peacefulness comes from nature to us and we return it to nature. There is no division between the gardener and the garden, so if the gardener feels peace within, so does the garden.

ARE YOU YOU?

"Height with a certain grace does bend,
But low things clownishly ascend."

One day the gardener noticed a man standing by her garden gate beckoning her over.

"Did you see me standing here?" he asked.

"Yes," the gardener replied.

"Have you ever seen me before?"

"No, I haven't."

"Then how do you know it was me?" he shouted before running off down the road.

"Thank you," said the gardener, returning to her weeding.

COMMENT

How do you know you are you? Of all the different roles you play, which if any is truly you, your being, your essence, your soul? Is it separate from your garden, from the earth – from anything?

Would you sell it, your essence, your soul? Would you disrespect your garden? If you were offered unlimited money, love and immortality would you sell your soul if it meant disrespecting and harming the earth?

The pressures of life, work, relationship, money, consumerism, and so on all add to the difficulty in staying on track with our deepest sense of who we are and what we want from life. Perhaps we all sell our souls when we do not follow the path which our deepest intuition and sense of self reveals to us. The gardener's relationship with her garden, with this beautiful earth, may bring her back to herself when she becomes caught up in this way.

The plants of the garden are at peace with the gardener for they appreciate the kind attention she gives to the garden, and the way she nourishes what nourishes them. They appreciate the times when she thins and prunes, weeds and replaces, for they know the spirit with which she performs all her acts in the garden, they know who she is. When she is receptive to their needs then her soul is nourished and her essence becomes one with the earth.

SEEING IN PROPORTION

"Casting the body's vest aside,
My soul into the boughs does glide."

One hot summer's day, as she was lying under a large apple tree in the garden, the gardener noticed the enormous marrows growing nearby.

"I wonder how is it," she mused to herself, "that such a large tree brings forth these small apples up in its branches compared to the scraggly, creeping marrow plant with produces such large fruits on the ground?"

As she was pondering this paradox, an apple fell and landed on her head.

"I see," the gardener exclaimed. "Now I know the reason why apples grow in the air and marrows on the ground! I should have thought of that before."

COMMENT

When you are aware of the planet, remember your garden. This beautiful earth is your biggest and best garden. It is vital we treat our biggest garden with the same care and attention we lavish on our own gardens. Of course, because of the greater scale, it is important we act in proportion to the tasks that are possible to us. If everyone in a garden fulfils their individual tasks, then the whole garden is cultivated and cared for just so.

People having a 'not in my back yard' attitude will move heaven and earth (as far as they are capable) to stop the construction of houses, of roads, and so on in what they consider as their back yard. The back yard becomes wider, the bigger the issue. Whilst at its own level this is commendable, it just pushes the issue elsewhere, into someone else's back yard. It is also a short-sighted attitude.

Everything has its place if only we work with each other and with nature. Not as simple as it sounds yet, at the same time, profoundly uncomplicated.

THE GARDEN GATE

"So architects do square and hew,
Green trees that in the forest grew."

The garden is a place for senses and sensing, sensing sights, smells, sounds, tastes and touch. Early in the morning the gardener likes to touch the ground and remember where she is, and she is touched too.

Reach out and touch the ground beneath you and then feel the ground touching you back. Close your eyes, place a hand on a tree and feel it touching you.

While boundaries are necessary they are all in the mind. Is that a lock upon my garden gate or just a snail passing by?

COMMENT

When you see your garden, see the planet. Consider how you apportion different amounts of energy to different jobs, you sow and you weed, you dig and you harvest. You plan and layout the garden, and at the same time the garden evolves. You control and you are controlled. All these different experiences are part of your on-going relationship with the garden. Sometimes you make mistakes, but you never intentionally harm anything. Even with weeds, your control in the garden does not stop them growing in the wild. They may well grow more vigorously there.

All boundaries are artificial. Of course we need garden fences and hedges. Yet what you do to your garden, you do to this beautiful earth. When you take the planet as your garden, then what you do to your garden, you do to the whole of existence. That is some responsibility, but of what value is gardening without it? Of what value is life itself without it? Response-ability is the mode for the gardener, never reacting to circumstance, always responding from the heart, where these values are held.

THE STUDENT

"Meantime, ye fields, springs, bushes, flowers,
Where yet she leads her studious hours."

When the gardener was a young student, she went to all the gardening lectures and took notes. She watched the television programmes about gardening and recorded them. She enrolled at the local horticultural college and was a most assiduous student. She wanted to learn the essence of gardening, to know what it was all really about.

As the years passed and her studies merely increased and increased, the gardener became more and more disillusioned. Finally one day she burned all of her notes, donated her videos to the local Oxfam shop, and resigned from college.

She went to live in a little house with a little garden and thought no more about learning the essence of gardening.

One day when she was digging her land, a small stone was dislodged by her spade, shot up and made a clang as it hit against a metal post that supported the compost heap.

At the moment the gardener heard the clang, "Aha!" she exclaimed, rolling on the ground, clutching at her sides as she laughed uproariously. "Now I understand. There is not much to this gardening after all!"

COMMENT

One of the main goddesses of the garden is Flora, but the garden is the abode of a multitude of gods and goddesses. Every flower is like a living deity. The beauty and wonder in this beautiful garden are insurmountable. Come and go in your garden. Get to see the impermanence of life. Be here now.

The garden itself is the best teacher. Then you can become all the gods and goddesses in the garden.

Leaving some of your garden wild provides refuge and home, perhaps for spirits and deities, but definitely for plants and animals. During the last forty years of the 20th Century, in Britain alone, ninety percent of wildflower meadows, eighty percent of downlands and over half of the woodlands disappeared. Well, not disappeared, they have been sprayed away, grubbed out, decimated by agribusiness, and so on. Some birds and frogs now literally depend on gardens to survive.

You're part of the wildlife yourself. Find a place for yourself in the garden, or watch your garden grow from the windows in your house. If you don't have your own garden, there are wonderful gardens, parks and open spaces that are equally part of this beautiful earth. Enjoy being in relationship with wildlife, sitting and looking at it, being the part of it you are.

GOOD TO BE IN

"In the green grass she loves to lie,
And there with her fair aspect tames
The wilder flowers, and gives them names."

A visitor, projecting his caught-up-ness onto the garden, walked its length without seeing a single yellow poppy. He missed the goldfinch that hopped before him and unthinkingly shooed away the red emperor butterfly that landed on his forearm.

"Why do you call this the garden of paradise?" he complained. "All I see is the time it must take you to keep it all in shape, and the money you spend on plants, and look, still there are weeds, still there are –

"Wait!" exclaimed the gardener. "Look. Listen. Don't you see, cannot you hear? What do you feel?"

"What?"

"When you realise this garden is neither good to be in nor bad to be in," she said, "you will experience this as the garden of paradise."

COMMENT

You do most gardening on your own, and then even the weeds can be company. The gardener remembers that weeds are just plants where you don't want them. If they are not doing any harm, they can be quite useful – like forget-me-nots. They will die back later but early in the year they fill spaces when not much else is around. They are weeds if you always take them out, pretty flowers if you use them. And some plants are always weeds in the garden, like the harmful bindweed wrapping round things or dandelions that take a lot of nutrients from the soil. This makes them no less part of this beautiful earth, though.

You can find weeds in your consciousness. After some time weeding, when you take a break, if you close your eyes then you can see the weeds right there. The gardener acknowledges this when digging them out. As Alexander Pope said:

"All nature is but art, unknown to thee;
All chance, direction which thou canst not see;
All discord, harmony not understood ...
One truth is clear, whatever is, is right."

IN THE MOMENT

"Thrice happy he who, not mistook,
Hath read in nature's mystick book."

The gardener was digging outside, and her neighbour asked her, "What are you working on?"

"Look," the gardener replied, pointing to the ground. "There's some excess soil here so I'm digging a hole to bury it in."

"So what are you going to do with the soil that you are digging out of the hole?" asked the neighbour.

"I can't attend to every single detail," she replied.

COMMENT

The way the gardener works is a practical example of her living in relationship with the garden even when she is unconscious of how she works. Nothing is taken as being wholly subjective or wholly objective otherwise one hole leads to another. Everything is itself and at the same time is all things. Digging or filling a hole, life is unfolding, everything becoming nothing and nothing becoming everything in the garden.

THE FORECAST

"So the all-seeing sun each day
Distils the world with chymick ray..."

The gardener said: "Look at the trees in the garden to recognize the power of the elements. The shape of the trees is the signature of the wind."

COMMENT

You leave your signature on your garden. As a child you are taught to write your name in a particular way, forming each letter carefully so that you learn to write clearly. As you became older, even if you write other things legibly, you usually write your signature in a way that is more to do with your character (or how you wish your character to be) than to do with how easily it will be read. For an older child and a teenager they look for an identity they try to express. This sticks and evolves. By middle age, most signatures are a scrawl that combines those early attempts you wish it to be with the dictates of time. It becomes an expression of the reality of who you are.

As you write your signature on your garden, you go through the same stages. The novice gardener works with care, following what it says in books or what they are told or shown. The 'teenage' gardener works at making the garden how he or she wishes it to be. The more experienced gardener trusts the process and signs the signature with a flourish but also with a careless abandon that allows the stroke of the pen to follow the tracks of time. It is not so much about control as co-operation with what is.

WINTERY WAYS

"When in the east the morning ray
Hangs out the colours of the day."

Stuck indoors and feeling depressed on a cold wintery day, the gardener reminded herself of the words of Camus: "In the depths of winter I finally learned that within me there lay an invincible summer."

"And it works just as well on a depressing summery day too," she thought, smiling and going back outdoors.

COMMENT

The gardener knows that a garden has a particular climate relating to the local area, which is part of a larger area, the region or district. The weather forecast might say it has been raining and in your garden its been sunny all afternoon. You may be in a mist whilst five miles away it is sunny. Weather is very particular to very small local areas and is constantly changing. Recognising the weather of your own garden is important to the gardener. You can use the forecasts on the internet, TV or in newspapers for the general trends of your area to help you make predictions. But you have to learn to make the best predictions for your garden.

It is also important to not always stay in when it's raining. There are things you can do. You don't want to clump about on the soil and compact it, that's not good for soil. Find all the other things you can do in the garden when its raining, whilst celebrating that rain is good for plants. Plants need water in right amounts, though – get too much and they can become waterlogged which can be worse than not getting enough.

Water in your garden has all sorts of things in it so spend some time to consider what has been put in intentionally or unintentionally, thoughtlessly or mindfully.

A CHANGING TALE

"You heaven's centre, nature's lap,
And paradise's only map."

When a friend asked the gardener if she was interested in philosophy she replied, "I garden, therefore I am. To garden is to dwell."

COMMENT

The wind drops, but the flower still falls; a bird sings, and the garden holds yet more mystery. When you are sitting quietly, doing nothing, spring comes and the grass just grows because it grows.

It is this inevitability of movement, of change, that is your one certainty. You do not know what will happen in the garden, except that it will change. A major task in gardening is not to work out this mystery, to not try to understand it, but to live with it and enjoy that not-knowing. All you can give the garden is your tenderness and your attention.

CORE AND COMPOST

"I have a garden of my own
But so with roses overgrown,
And lilies, that you would it guess
To be a little wilderness."

The gardener smiled as her friend marvelled at the cycles of life in the garden. "Yes, my friend," she said, "and remember that one day you too will become compost and feed our little friends."

COMMENT

On a wet day when you hear the raindrops falling, hear the rain as tears of grief and realise it is sadness inside that makes you hear them that way. If you hear the rain as thunderous applause praising your successful planting, it is the bloated one inside you who makes it seem so. The same applies to all aspects of your relationship with garden. You can easily project your own feelings and emotional reactions onto the garden as a whole, or aspects and areas of the garden. You feel angry at those weeds for growing again where you cleared the soil for planting. You feel sad for the pear tree that has lost its partner. You know the new little tomato seedlings, pushing up through the soil with such fragility, fear the wind and rain. The blossoming apple expresses such joy.

The plants within the garden do not experience these feelings. They just simply are what they are. They are born, they grow and they die (and return to the garden in which all is slowly or ultimately recycled). From earth and returned to earth: this is not sad or joyous, it just is.

It is this realisation that brings you closer to the core. It is within this experience that you can truly enjoy and be sad over your losses, knowing they are your responses which will also be born, grow and then die. That which remains is the garden itself of which you are a part.

What the gardener said is true: you too will become compost and feed your little friends.

THE FIRST TIME

"What wondrous life is this I lead!
Ripe apples drop about my head."

In summer, the gardener loves the opportunity to roll naked, in moonlight, on a patch of bare earth previously warmed by the sun. It is an experience not to be missed!

COMMENT

The first time of walking with bare feet in the garden each year is a highlight of early Spring. A sunny day, take off your shoes and socks and put your bare feet onto the grass. Feel its tickle. Stand up and feel your weight resting firmly on this beautiful earth. If it is a little damp, so much the better.

Allow the grass to massage the bottom of your feet. Let the healing properties of the grass be transmitted up your legs. When you feel ready, sit down and, if you can, let your feet dry and warm in the sunlight. (Otherwise, wrap your feet up to keep them warm.) Feel the energy now flowing up through your legs, up your body, and right out the top of your head.

TO TOUCH THE GRASS

"And now to the abyss I pass,
Of that unfathomable grass."

The gardener admired a magnificent lawn in a country estate, green and perfect and soft and velvety. She went over and asked the groundsman who was watering it: "What is the secret of making a lawn like this?"

"Ah, it's no secret," replied the groundsman. "I don't mind telling you."

"Marvellous," said the gardener. "I'll make my lawn at home as fine as this."

"The method," said the groundsman, "is merely to plant a lawn, remove the weeds, keep it flat and smooth, and make sure you cut the grass frequently."

"That's easy enough,' said the gardener. "And how long does it take to get in this condition?"

"About two to three hundred years, madam."

"Hmm," responded the gardener. "In that case we like our lawn at home after all – with all its weeds and bumps – thank you very much anyway!"

COMMENT

The gardener remembers that everything we do in the garden is part of a cycle. The art of gardening is in flowing with this cycle, trusting the unfoldment of the process. The grass growing of itself is only half the story. The grass also needs trimming of itself and this action is what transforms the wild into the garden. By doing both – interrupting the flow of nature or going with the flow of nature at the same time – the gardener creates.

The gardener, when sitting quietly, does nothing; and when gardening intently, does everything. What is vital is to be both everything and nothing – the being and the doing. Then as Emerson mused: "And the poor grass shall plot and plan, What it will do when it is man."

BEAUTIFUL NEIGHBOURS

"For he did, with his utmost skill,
Ambition weed, but conscience till."

One day a neighbour wanted to borrow the spade.

"Sorry," said the gardener, "I am using it to prune a rosebush."

"How on earth can you prune a rosebush with a spade?" asked the neighbour.

The gardener replied: "Well, it is less difficult than you'd imagine when you don't want to lend it."

COMMENT

Once upon a time there were two neighbours who loved each other very much. One of them, called Tom, lived with his wife and two daughters. The other was Tim, and he lived alone. Whenever Tom had a crop in more abundance than Tim, he would take from his basket and slip it into his neighbour's. After all, thought Tom, poor Tim lives alone. Tim always did the same – after all, he thought, Tom has a family to feed. In this way they both experienced abundance, and lived happily as neighbours. Then one day Tom caught Tim putting carrots into his basket at exactly the same moment he was putting some radishes into Tim's basket! How they laughed as they realised what they had always done.

There are ancient versions of this story in which God sees this neighbourly harmony and blesses the two gardens. Thereafter these gardens become a sacred shrine and many people visit to wonder at their beauty. In the story of Tom and Tim the same thing happens. Because of their kindliness in sharing with each other, their gardens do become truly beautiful and people experience joy when they walk in them.

So now we know: 'kindliness in sharing' is God. So as well as cultivating your garden, it is vital you also cultivate your neighbours as part of an on-going process, not a one-off event.

Be mindful of the words of Basho, the Japanese Haiku poet, who wrote:

"It is deep autumn;
My neighbour –
How does he live, I wonder?"

THE FROG'S RETURN

"Till as a crystal mirror slick,
Where all things gaze themselves, and doubt
If they be in it or without."

The gardener saw the first frog sitting on a leaf in the pond, sunning himself, his eyes and nose pointing towards the afternoon sun. Such a delight! It is the first sign of summer, when the frogs come back to the pond, joining the fish. Their natural, animal presence brings wholeness to the eco-system of the pond.

A second frog becomes visible. "Look, there!" exclaimed the gardener, pointing at the small frog sitting just to one side of the big one. Time stilled as she look into the small frog's beautiful eye, ringed with bright gold, glowing in the sunshine.

"What is the sound of one frog jumping?"

COMMENT

Basho wrote another classic Haiku, perhaps the most famous of all:

> The old pond;
> A frog jumps in –
> The sound of the water.

All haiku poetry is simple and immediate and provokes us to stop and assess a moment of life through its subject. Haiku poems often reveal to us that something – by implication, everything – exists at one and the same time outside and inside the mind. Being in the moment, a haiku is not concerned for what has been or what will be. Life is impermanent but meaning can be found in each passing moment if we stop to consider it. There is then nothing to explain and no time in which to explain it.

A haiku poem speaks to our 'not-self' – it is only our illusion of a separate self that gets us caught up in emotional knots; without a self we identify with this beautiful earth, we relax into it, and can live more compassionately, at one with the fate of all creatures including ourselves.

Three lines, any length, no explanation, just a moment in time. For instance:

> How a small snail
> Climbs a blade of grass –
> But slowly, slowly …

Now your turn:

SMALL AND LARGE

"And, oh, so close your circles lace,
That I may never leave this place."

If you hide something small in a very large place, like a needle in a haystack, you may consider it safe. But it can be found. The clever hunter always finds what she looks for. With the haystack, for instance, she may burn it down to discover the needle within.

On the other hand, if you hide something large in something small it is much harder to find, although it may be clearly visible.

Beyond this, if you hide the universe in the universe itself, there is no place for it to be found as there is no place for it to be lost. Thus it is for the planting of a garden.

We wouldn't be here at all if we didn't have the earth to support the biosphere in which we live. In respecting our planet we respect ourselves. Further, we add to the flow of positive energies that counteract the negative which brings abuse, famine, war and so on. In respecting our planet, we are co-operating with the unfoldment of life, and passing on to the next generation a place at least as good to live in and perhaps better. There is another sometimes overlooked benefit, too. When we align ourselves and co-operate with earth energies, our good will is returned to us.

A gardener considers the longevity of different species, those things that last a short time, maybe only a day in bloom, compared to those that last forever (including weeds!) Consider your longevity and that you might die very soon. Where would you rather be but in this beautiful garden?

Edward Lear understood when he wrote: "There was an old man who said, "Hush! I perceive a young bird in a bush!" When they said, "Is it small," he replied, "Not at all; it is four times as big as the bush!"

A DILEMMA

"A prickling leaf it bears, and such
As that which shrinks at every touch;
But flowers eternal, and divine,
That in the crowns of saints do shine."

The gardener planted a sage bush and it grew wide and strong, bearing beautiful purple flowers at the beginning of the summer. But amidst its stems and roots grew the creepy lesser celandine. The roots and rootlets of the sage and the celandine intertwined, and she could not weed out the celandine without possibly injuring the sage. And when she watered and nourished the sage she did the same for the celandine.

The gardener said: "This is really no problem at all for the celandine dies down before the sage comes into flower anyway. First there is a mountain, then there isn't."

COMMENT

Then there is.

Sometimes you speak, sometimes you are silent. Sometimes this exists, sometimes that. You are alone and then you are not.

This is the existential situation, a dilemma of the practical world that can only be solved through living, through co-creating with this beautiful earth and witnessing the interaction.

THE TREES

"Fair trees! wheresoe'er your barks I wound,
No name shall but your own be found."

The gardener was walking in the garden with a friend when they came to the twisted, bulbous tree at the bottom of the northern slope. "The trunk of this tree is so twisted, it has all these bulbous growths, the branches are contorted." The gardener smiled. "To a carpenter this tree is useless, but to a gardener it is a delight."

"Yes," says the visitor. "It is truly magnificent that there is no way for it to be used, which ensures it comes to no harm. You couldn't make planks or posts out of it, for instance."

"But we may slumber under its branches in the heat of the midsummer sun!" exclaimed the gardener. "It is planted in the region of not-doing, that's why. At that time, we wander beside it in a state of non-action."

COMMENT

The pine tree stands straight, reaching up to the sky, aiming for one hundred feet tall or more. The daisy stands just above the grass, an inch or so of visibility above the blanket of green. Both live within the same garden, each with its share of length and shortness. The length of the pine tree just is, just as the shortness of the daisy cannot be changed. To realise this in the garden is to rise above the petty tyranny of aiming for an unnatural perfection.

SHADOW AND LIGHT

"So when the shadows laid asleep
From underneath these banks do creep."

The gardener said: "When the spring blossoms fade and fall, we know it is the end of spring. Yet in all endings are beginnings. Now the garden is wider, it is fuller and it holds more shadow."

COMMENT

The end of late spring is the beginning of early summer. All the leaves are coming out on the trees, the grass is pushing up, the summer plants are increasing, and the vegetables are growing rapidly. During the winter there was much space in the garden – what light there was played around the bare branches and filled the garden. Now as the garden fills with more plants that are richer and more luxurious, although there is more light (from the summer sun) there are more places where the sun cannot reach. Many of the plants like this, love this indeed. For these plants, too much undiluted sunshine is death, they would dry up and shrivel.

To work the garden you have to consider the interplay of light and dark. As with life, if you try to deny the shadow aspects of your existence you will be partial and incomplete, so with the garden, which needs the shadows to promote growth. The shadows also make the brightness more enjoyable. After working in the sunshine what joy to relax in a shady place, feeling the warm air filled with the summer scents. After relaxing in the hot summer sun, who does not appreciate the shady grove in which to work? This is true for plants too.

In all endings are beginnings. Such is the cyclical nature of life and gardening. No light exists without casting shadows. You exist within these cycles, within these polarities, as do all the plants within the garden. Acceptance of this is necessary for your existence to be full. By the same token, your garden is fuller when you acknowledge the patterns of light and dark, growth and decay.

MY CHILD AND I

"And fauns and fairies do the meadows till,
More by their presence than their skill."

The gardener and her child don't worry about what is 'proper.' They just want to plunge their hands into the earth, dig, plant, weed, moan, groan and thoroughly enjoy.

COMMENT

The gardener takes her inner child into the garden every time she enters there. She may not always acknowledge the child, or even remember that he is there. Yet she is in active dialogue with him about the fun and joy of living.

At the same time, she will contain him. Sometimes children want to dig plants out that it would be better to leave in place. Sometimes they are unable to see what is around them, being so preoccupied with something or another. At these and similar times, the gardener needs to be aware of the child, to stop him from inappropriately destroying something.

How important then for the gardener to choose to be with the child at other times – ordinary, chore-filled gardening times like when you are beset with too, too many weeds in spring. And joy filled times of engagement such as when you are deeply involved in planting seeds. And times of wonder like when you are carried away with the beauty of a sweet-scented, deep red rose. When the gardener shares her appreciation of the garden with her child, then the relationship with him brings harmonious energies into the garden.

Also there are times not to have the child in the garden. When you stop talking, become silent and enter the world of dreaming, at those times, in your silence, you hear the heartbeat of the garden. And a bird sings.

BUDDHA, GNOME, GODDESS

"'Tis she that to these gardens gave
That wondrous beauty which they have."

The gardener says: "Pick one blade of grass and see it as a ten foot, golden Buddha."

COMMENT

Representations with spiritual meaning can invigorate your heart. A stone Buddha, seated amidst colourful flowers, can be very grounding, can bring great peace to your garden. In summer the stone Buddha sizzles with the heat, and the glare of the sun on its white surface is enough to remind you of the transience of life, to stop and enjoy the warmth whilst you may. At other times, sometimes wet, sometimes dry, its presence acts as a reminder that these things too will pass. And there is also that which remains.

For some people it is gnomes, painted red and sitting amidst the grass with a plastic fishing rod. A cliché can also connect you to an archetype. After all, there are real gnomes in the garden. At dusk, caught in the corner of your eye, the garden gnome can sometimes be seen scurrying about his business.

But the goddess of this beautiful earth is always present – in the soil, the plants, the leaves, the flowers, the air surrounding. And each blade of grass has the presence of a Buddha when seen with the eyes of a gardener.

One blade of grass is no different from Buddha so your garden is populated by a countless multitude of Buddhas which are all one Buddha. As they say: many blades of grass, one lawn.

NOT GARDENING

*"How well the skilful gardener drew
Of flowers and herbs this dial new."*

The gardener said, "The whole garden is covered by the snow. Nothing remains."

To which her friend replied: "Come inside!"

COMMENT

There is something to be done in the garden every day of the year, but on those short, cold wintry days when the weather just doesn't allow you to go outside, you have many choices as a gardener. You can look through the seed catalogues and plan the next summer's garden; you can do something else completely different not connected to gardening at all.

Or you can go outside anyway.

Whichever choice you make, you are all ways co-operating with the garden. The plants, the insects, the soil – all the other beings in the garden may make these choices about you, too.

THE CROOKED STRAW HAT

"Do you, O brambles, chain me too,
And courteous briars, nail me through."

"When I work with the rake," said the gardener, "and set to raking,
I always find my straw hat on crooked."

COMMENT

Whilst raking the grass, the gardener makes one movement repeated over and over with infinitesimally different strokes, and she is either absent or present. Absent, thinking about other things or lost in an emotional response to some past pain. Present, not thinking, not reacting, simply stroking the rake across the grass. Then the raker and rake become one with the grass.

INTO THE MYSTIC

"Your sacred plants, if here below,
Only among the plants will grow. "

One day a mystic visited the garden. "At my teaching centre," he said, "the more people know, the harder the tasks I give them. You must be the know-all in this garden."

"It's a good job I know nothing, then," said the gardener, laughing.

"But you do know something," said the mystic in a serious voice. "You know the difference between Work (with a capital W)" – he said it over loudly to emphasise the difference, – "and work with a small 'w'."

Later that day, as they were working together in the vegetable patch, the mystic said to the gardener: "I've only recently started gardening. Please teach me."

The gardener asked: "Have you hoed between the vegetable rows?"

"I have," replied the mystic.

"Then you had better clean your hoe."

At that moment the mystic understood the essence of gardening.

COMMENT

Working in the garden includes both working in the garden and playing in the garden. Your garden testifies to that whether you are aware of it or not. So the point is to be mindful of what defines work in your life. Be like the so-called indigenous peoples, recognising soul in everyday things, in your relationship with the garden. Don't see yourselves as separate or superior to nature. Recognize the interdependence of all creation and honour it.

LONG LOVE'S DAY

"The grave's a fine and private place,
But none, I think, do there embrace."

The gardener asked herself: "Whilst you were gardening today, what was happening?" ... and reminded herself of the words of the poet Kahlil Gibran who said that work is love made visible, to work is to sow seeds with tenderness and reap the harvest with joy, even as if your beloved were to eat the fruit.

COMMENT

What was happening? Not a lot in one way, and at the same time you have travelled many millions of miles in space, many thousands of babies were born, many thousands of people died.

You cannot change that, all you can do is accept what is. You are always in the present, you cannot live in the past or exist in the future. The only place you exist is in the present moment.

You are always here and now: here in this particular garden and now at this particular time. In this moment of time – in any moment of time – in every garden, what remains the same is not what you perceive, nor what is existing in the garden. What remains the same is the attention you bring to that which you perceive. As you look at the garden you can start to accept yourself as being the source of what you perceive and what happens in the garden.

Yet paradoxically you cannot find this space within you nor fix it in time.

VEGETABLES IN THE SACK

"Stumbling on melons, as I pass,
Ensnared with flowers, I fall on grass."

Entering the garden one day, the gardener saw a man there filling his sack with all the vegetables he could lay his hands on.

The gardener shouted: "What are you doing here?"

"I was blown here by a high wind," responded the man, standing up and facing her.

"And who uprooted the vegetables?"

"I caught hold of them to stop myself being swept along," replied the man.

"And how does it come, then," said the gardener, "that there are vegetables in that sack beside you?"

"Hmm," said the man. "That is just what I was wondering when you came into the garden."

They both laughed and the gardener helped him fill the rest of his sack before going along his way.

COMMENT

You live in a beautiful garden on this beautiful earth. If you ask where is this beautiful garden, you are not in touch with where you are. In a single-roomed apartment without a garden (or even a window box), you can be in this beautiful garden. Or you can be in the most colourful and well laid-out country garden and not be there. This beautiful garden is all around you if you remember, and choose. This beautiful garden is what you create – in your garden, around you on the planet, and in your life. Yet metaphors are most real when applied, so this beautiful earth is also what you create when you get out the gardening tools and work in a real, physical garden. Like the one at the back of your house, perhaps. Like the one that is your life, certainly.

A GARDEN OF LIGHT

"Meanwhile the mind, from pleasure less,
Withdraws into its happiness."

Make yourself comfortable and let your attention turn inwards.
Watch your breath as it comes into your body, turns then passes
right out again. Let go of any tensions as you breathe out. Imagine
you are standing in your garden, facing the sun, which is gently
warming your face. (Even if your garden does not get any sun, in
your imagination it can have as much sunshine as you want.)

You can hear birds singing, and in the distance you can
hear the faint voices of children, happily playing. You feel your
body relax.

As the sun warms your face, it also warms your chest. As
it does so, you become aware of your heart. A bird chirps nearby,
sharing your stillness. You take a deep breath – do it – and feel
your heart open to the warmth of the sun. There is a tingling
of pleasure in your legs as you feel yourself firmly root into the
warm, nourishing earth.

You turn your face up to the sun as you enter a deeper
silence, a stillness in which your heart is bathed with light and
healing energies...

Breathe the healing light into your heart, open your eyes
and:

Become a gardener in the garden of life on this beautiful earth.

FINALLY...

A visitor to the garden once asked the gardener, "What is the best plant in the whole garden?"

"Everything in my garden is the best," replied the gardener. "You cannot find here any plant that is not the best."

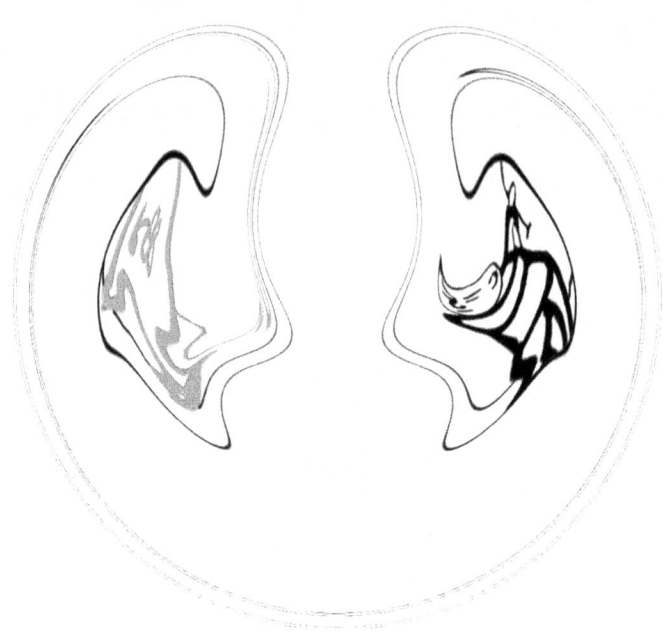

The Ten Bulls illustrations are based on a Taoist text from China originating more than two thousand years ago. Although its origins are lost, it has been used extensively by Taoists and Zen Buddhists to illustrate the stages on a journey towards enlightenment and the subsequent return to the world afterwards. It has been adapted in many ways, both spiritual and secular, and is widely available in various forms in books and on the internet.

Anyone who has ever had a cow loose in their garden will know what devastation they can quickly cause; it's a projection of course, but they do look like they are actually enjoying trampling your veg and chewing on bushes! There's a wild look in their eyes. But this is rare – very few people actually experience having a large animal like a cow rampage in their garden.

But there is a 'bull' in the garden – the continuous work, the search for perfection – or at least completion. One task always leads to another; as soon as one area is weeded another is needing attention, and so on. The following adaptation of the original Ten Bulls renames the 'bull' as 'the perfect gardener' but consider: who or what is the "bull" in your garden?

The following illustrations are a homage to Tomikichiro Tokuriki, one of Japan's greatest artists, whose timeless and evocative oxherding pictures inspired my attempts.

1. THE SEARCH FOR THE PERFECT GARDENER

In the garden I endlessly mow the ever-growing grass in search of becoming the perfect gardener.

Walking around various flower beds, lost upon interpenetrating paths across the lawn, my strength failing and my vitality exhausted, I have not become the perfect gardener. There is no end, there is always more to do.

I hear only the bees buzzing through the late afternoon.

COMMENT

This is the most difficult path for the way ahead is unknown. Why try to be a perfect gardener at all? Is the search already completed, though hardly begun? Has perfection ever been lost? Where can you look?

2. DISCOVERING THE WAY AHEAD

Around the pond side, under a tree, I catch a glimpse of the next step.

Then across the fragrant grass I see potential. Even around the compost heap it is found.

These traces can be no more hidden than your nose.

COMMENT

You see the way ahead – as soon as you start looking, the signs are seen everywhere. Where does it lead? Mind your step, your very next step. Does this explain everything – or nothing? How do you see the path ahead?

3. PERCEIVING THE POSSIBILITY

I hear the song of the thrush.

The sun is warm, the wind is mild, leaves are full and are green throughout the garden. Now the garden feels open and beautiful.

What gardener can keep it this way, that trimmed lawn, those beautiful lilies?

COMMENT

Do you see yourself as the perfect gardener? Where can it be beyond the mind? The garden is strong and self-contained, so what does it offer you? What do you offer to it?

4. TENDING THE GARDEN

It's a terrific struggle to keep the garden tidy. The work needed for this is exhausting.

The possibility of being a perfect gardener is as far away as a high plateau far above cloud mists ...

...or lost deep in an inpenetratable ravine of lost chances.

COMMENT

Even if you were to reach the centre, would the garden now be perfect? The large country garden and the small window box – which can you tend?

5. TAMING THE GARDEN

The hoe and shears are necessary, else the garden will become overgrown, dusty and forgotten.

Being well trained, I do all that is necessary and more.

The garden remains free and not controllable.

COMMENT

Who needs the taming? Whose life is in the scales? Where can you balance?

6. THE MUSIC OF THE GARDEN

Relaxing, I slowly realise what I need to not do.

After placing the gardening tools in the shed, the voice of my flute intones through the evening. Measuring with hand beats the pulsating harmony, I enjoy endless rhythm.

My flute, the song of the thrush, the burrowing of worms, there is no distinction now.

COMMENT

The garden is tamed, you relax and play, what more is there? King or queen of the jungle, are you content?

7. THE GARDEN TRANSCENDED

Beyond struggle and work, I reach the centre.

I am serene, and now the garden too can rest.

The sunset has come and in blissful repose, I enter the house and let go of the day's chores.

COMMENT

Is there a path? Was there ever any path? Have you ever left home? Have you ever anywhere to go? Do you see? Who are you?

8. BOTH GARDEN AND SELF TRANSCENDED

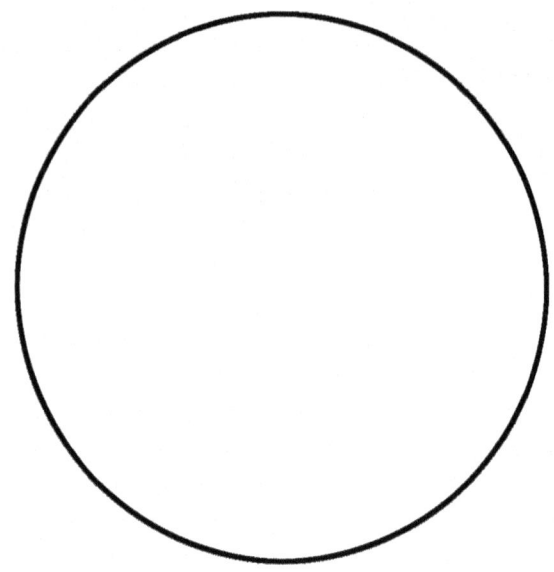

Everything, tools, plants, lawn, compost, all merge into No-Thing.

This dream is so vast there is no need of a message.

How may a snowflake exist in a raging fire except in dreaming?

COMMENT

What is left? Is there any limitation left? Is there meaning? An open door to step through into a part of the whole that is no longer apart?

9. REACHING THE SOURCE

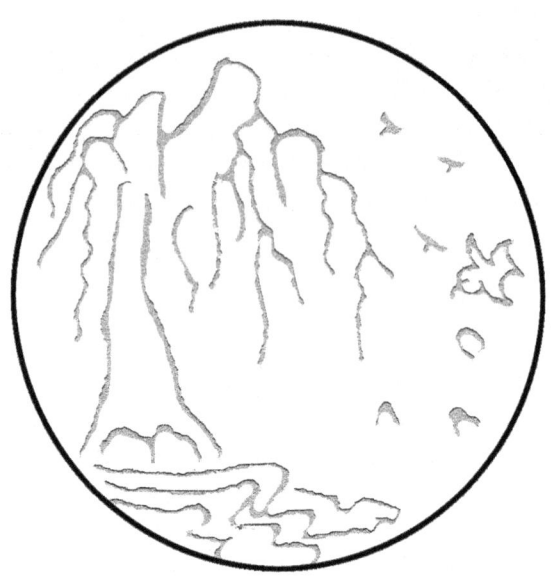

Too much work has been undertaken returning to the root and source. Better to have been relaxed and easy from the beginning.

Dwelling in my true abode, unconcerned with that without, the garden simply grows and the flowers are coloured by themselves.

COMMENT

If no steps are too few and one step is too many how should you tread? Are you foolish or wise? Are you? Air gives us life but we do not see it. Gentle petals flutter in the breeze – what moves: petals, air or mind?

10. BACK IN THE GARDEN

Barefoot and naked of breast, I enter the early morning garden on a new day.

The sun shines on both the garden and my body, and I am ever blissful.

I have no need to struggle with the garden, no need to be the perfect gardener: now, before me, even dead trees become alive.

COMMENT

As above so below, as within so without. Were the trees ever alive or dead? Who is enlightened? Who is not? Who is the perfect gardener? The beauty of my garden is visible for all to see, and everyone I look upon is enlightened.

Lightning Source UK Ltd.
Milton Keynes UK
UKOW04f2343271217
315163UK00001BA/184/P

9 780957 224674